W9-AFM-392

COMPANIONABLE
BOOKS

By

GEORGE GORDON

MERTON PROFESSOR OF ENGLISH LITERATURE

IN THE UNIVERSITY OF

OXFORD

SERIES I

ST. JOSEPH'S UNIVERSITY STX

PR99.G66C

Companionable books.

3 9353 00032 9753

PR 99
.G66C

ESSAY INDEX

Essay Index Reprint Series

91066

 BOOKS FOR LIBRARIES PRESS
FREEPORT, NEW YORK

First Published 1927
Reprinted 1968

LIBRARY OF CONGRESS CATALOG CARD NUMBER:

68-16935

PRINTED IN THE UNITED STATES OF AMERICA

PREFACE

THESE short and unpretending discourses are published in obedience to requests the number and warmth of which surprised me. They were delivered at the invitation of the British Broadcasting Company, principally in November and December of 1926, and though I understood at the time that they were thought to serve a purpose, I was unprepared to discover that so many who approved of them as listeners were ready to endure them in print. My first thought, in the circumstances, was to publish them as they stood. My second, which I have acted on, was to revise them, and to add some things which the time limits of broadcasting had obliged me to omit. The general result, I hope, is an improvement. But I have done nothing to alter their original character. They were planned as Talks, and Talks I have been careful to leave them.

The first six made a series, and the description of the series, ' Companionable Books,' has been retained in the title. The seventh, on Charles Lamb, though of earlier date and without serial connection, has been thought sufficiently in harmony to be included.

Their purpose, when they were delivered, was this. There are a great many people who shrink from opening an old book because it is old. There are almost as many who, if you present them with a book, and tell them it is a literary masterpiece, at once show signs of panic, and are evidently afraid to be left alone with it. If it is old, they think it is probably dull ; and if it is a masterpiece, they are sure it will be over their heads. I hoped to convince such persons, if they would do me the honour to listen to me, that about some old books, at any rate, they were making a mistake, and were missing, in fact, a great deal of pleasure. The books I chose to talk about were none of them modern, and I did not deny that they were masterpieces of their kind. But I ventured to assert that they were, every one of them, much more alive and a great deal more companionable than any best seller one might care to name. What most men and women are looking for all their lives is companionship, and so far as books provide it, here it was. There is a companionable quality in some books that skips the centuries, and I was reluctant that any one should miss it through mere timidity and misunderstanding. My efforts had some result. At any rate, a good many bought the books, and some have written to say that I did not exaggerate.

The chief difficulty in broadcasting is that one cannot choose one's audience. I was addressing myself primarily to the uninitiated, to that large body of sensible but unliterary people whose knowledge of books is confined for the most part to the books of their own time. But my audience, as I was to learn, contained others, already perfectly acquainted with the works on which I was expatiating, and only curious to compare notes or to observe how I should acquit myself. It was a relief to be assured by some of these initiates that what was meant for the majority had on the whole survived their tests.

I have had many inquiries about editions. The only complete edition of Pepys's *Diary* is that published by Messrs. G. Bell and Sons ; it can now be had in three volumes. The best selection from the *Diary* is Mr. Morshead's *Everybody's Pepys*, recently issued in one volume by the same publishers. The *Complete Angler*, Boswell's *Life*, and *Tristram Shandy* can all be

bought for a few shillings in such series as
'The World's Classics,' the 'Oxford Standard
Authors,' or 'Everyman's Library.' The
Oxford University Press even publishes the
Angler as a Thumb Classic : '128mo :
$2\frac{1}{2} \times 1\frac{3}{4} \times \frac{3}{8}$ inches ' ! Cowper's Letters do not
lend themselves to such a miracle. The
standard edition is by Thomas Wright (of the
Cowper School, Olney), in four volumes
(1904) ; but good selections are to be had,
notably Sir James Frazer's, in two volumes
(1912), and Mr. E. V. Lucas's in the cheaper
form of 'The World's Classics.' Of *Eothen* I
can name no better edition than Mr. Hogarth's,
published, in their 'Oxford Miscellany'
Series, by the Oxford University Press.

GEORGE GORDON.

CONTENTS

COMPANIONABLE BOOKS

PEPYS'S DIARY

THE most important thing about Pepys's
Diary is that we were never meant to
see it. There 's interest for you ! Every reader
of Pepys enjoys, that is to say, from start to
finish, ' the fearful pleasures of the keyhole '—
of seeing and hearing what he was never intended to see or hear. Pepys took great pre-
cautions : wrote it in shorthand (with various
dodges to make the script more difficult), and
wrote it in his office after hours, when all the
clerks had gone. He kept it locked up there ;
for if he had taken it home, his wife, ' poor
wretch,' as he calls her, might have asked
questions. He carried it on for eight and a half
years, till his eyes grew weak,—from 1660, when
he was twenty-seven, to 1669, when he was
thirty-six,—putting down all his doings, and all
his little motives, with perfect honesty. There
is hardly an erasure in his script : down it
went, and stood there. The result is the
frankest and most intimate book in print.

How it should have survived is the puzzle ;

why, in old age, retired from business, full of honours and respectability, he did not destroy it. On the contrary, he had the six volumes bound uniformly with the rest of his library. They were a part of his life, and he could not bring himself to efface them. Perhaps he thought the script would deter readers ; and so it did for more than a century. Then some one thought of deciphering a page, and the result was so interesting that it clearly could not stop there. The three thousand pages took three years to decode, and eventually, in 1825, a selection was published. The readers of that day could hardly believe their luck, and Macaulay woke in a cold sweat after dreaming that it was a forgery. But their luck was nothing to ours. Though they did not suspect it, barely half the *Diary* had been printed. Since then, bit by bit, as public taste grew less prudish, the complete record has appeared, and it may reasonably be said that we possess it all.

The first thing we note about the *Diary* is that it puts every reader in a good humour. For, in the first place, Pepys himself enjoys everything so much : his clothes, his house, his work, his jaunts, the respect people paid him, the pretty women he saw and the pretty women he kissed, the music he heard and the music he made, the theatre, his dinner parties, his books, and not least—indeed the condition of all the rest—his steadily increasing bank balance. For money, as he says, ' sweetens everything.' His enjoyment of them all is so whole-hearted and childlike that we enjoy them with him.

He not only puts one in a good humour generally, but in a good humour with oneself. Some books humiliate us with a sense of our inferiority to the great men who wrote them. But almost every one is superior to Pepys in some respect. He was a better business man than most of us—the best Secretary the Admiralty had ever had. But then, he took presents, and little commissions on contracts, which of course you and I would never do. He was as fond of his wife as most husbands ; but, I regret to say it, he was even fonder sometimes of the wives of others. He could have taught most of us something about music ; but, on the other hand, he drank too much, and was so ' foxed ' occasionally that he daren't read family prayers. He was an excellent householder and a generous host, and believed in having everything neat and handsome about him. But it is glaringly evident that he spent a great deal more on himself than on his wife : and besides, he blacked her eye once, and pulled her nose twice, and beat his servants—all of which, of course, is very terrible. He was a leading book-collector, and the library he left is one of the jewels of its kind : specially housed in his old college at Cambridge, visited from all parts of the world, and with a special librarian to look after it. But we can still feel superior when we find that he thought most of Shakespeare silly, and failed in every attempt to see the joke of *Hudibras*. He was President of the Royal Society in his later years ; but he believed (and here again we score) that if you drown a negro he turns white, that a hare's foot is a charm for the colic, and that a very high wind means that some great person is about to die. In the terrible Plague year of 1665 he was one of the few officials who stayed on in London and saw it through ; but just as we are commending him for his pluck and public spirit he breaks in with the remark that it was, in fact, the best year he had ever had —because he made more money that year than ever before.

What a mixture it is ! And what a lesson on human complexity ! Pepys's public reputation suffered heavily when the *Diary* first appeared. But if we all kept a diary like Pepys, and were as completely frank ; if we put down not only all we did, but all (really all) that on every occasion we should have liked to do, if respectability or self-interest had not forbidden it ; if we noted all our motives (not only the generous fine ones, but all the little mean ones that run mocking at the others' heels), should we not present—even the best of us—a rather mixed spectacle too ? Public opinion has come round. Pepys's serious achievements are respected as much as ever, and his foibles and his candour have made him loved. Every man can see himself, or his neighbour, in Pepys's *Diary*, as it were through the back-door.

If there is a business man in England who has not read this Diary, let me advise him to take the first opportunity of doing so. I say business man, because it is above all things the diary of a rising young man of business, and one of the chief pleasures of it is to see him rise. He had married for love, without a halfpenny, when he was twenty-two and she was fifteen, and when we first meet them, five years later, they are just beginning to be established, with one maid and a dog. Strict economy was their rule, and they never refused an invitation to dinner. On 29th January 1660 we are privileged to look on at his first monthly balance : I ' do find myself to be worth £40 and more,' he writes, ' which I did not think, but am afraid that I have forgot something.' Here is a feeling that we all have shared ! The £40 in due course becomes £100 ; then £200, and he gives his wife a necklace ; and he ends the first year with £300 and all debts paid, for which ' Blessed be Almighty God ! ' An uncle dies : ' so I rose sorry in some respects, glad in my expectations in another respect ' ; and he goes down to the funeral soberly enough, but ' greedy to see the will.' When he reaches £500 he talks in bed to his wife of what he will do when he has £2000 : ' be a Knight, my dear, and keep my coach, which pleased her.' Before the *Diary* closes he is well on his way to the £10,000 mark (which would be nearer £50,000 now), and had his coach, though not his knighthood : ' and what pleasure to go alone with my poor wife in a coach of our own to see a play, and makes us appear mighty great, I think, in the world ; at least, greater than ever I could, or my friends for me, have once expected.' Pepys, you see, like Mr. Wells's William Clissold, believed in travelling by ' the blue train.' He also believed in work. Vain as he was, and self-important, he had no illusions about that. ' For myself,' he says, ' chance without merit brought me in, and . . . diligence only keeps me so ; and will, living as I do among so many lazy people.'

At home Pepys was master—as much as he dared. Let me recommend his Diary to every married man and woman who has any leisure for reading, as a picture,—one of the most amusing and unabashed ever drawn,—of married life from the husband's point of view. All the usual home troubles of a husband will be found there. He hit his thumb with a hammer when he was knocking in pegs. He put it out when chastising an idle servant boy. And by an unfortunate choice of time and place he struck the cookmaid ' in our entry,' with one of his neighbour's domestics looking on, 'which did vex me to the heart because I know he will be telling their family of it.'

Twentieth century householders have many better reasons for not hitting their cooks, but they will none the less appreciate Pepys's natural vexation at having his performance watched. It was a footboy who saw him, and ' I did put on presently,' he says, ' a very pleasant face to the boy and spoke kindly to him, as one without passion, so as it may be he might not think I was angry ; but yet I was troubled at it.'

His relations with his wife were more complicated. Pepys was a very tidy man, and his wife the reverse, and there were scenes. ' Angry with my wife for her things lying about, and in my passion kicked the little fine basket which I bought her in Holland, and broke it, which troubled me after I had done it.' ' Dined at home, discontented that my wife do not go neater now she has two maids.' ' Home to dinner, where finding the cloth laid and much crumpled, but clean, I grew angry and flung the trenchers about the room, and in a mighty heat I was. So a clean cloth was laid, and my poor wife very patient.' No doubt he was often unreasonable, as husbands are. ' Thence my wife and I home, and found all well, only myself somewhat vexed at my wife's neglect in leaving of her scarf, waist-coat and night-dressings in the coach to-day that brought us from Westminster ; though, I confess, she did give them to me to look after, yet it was her fault not to see that I did take them out of the coach.' There is a familiar ring about this which I need not emphasise.

But the chief ground of contention was Pepys's kindly eye for women. ' Music and women,' he confesses, ' I cannot but give way to, whatever my business is.' He could never resist a pretty face, and, shrewd as he was, dealt always with the shops with the prettiest girls in them. ' Called upon Doll . . . for a pair of gloves . . . which cost me 20s., but she is so pretty that, God forgive me, I could not think it much : which is a strange slavery that I stand in to beauty, that I value nothing near it.' ' To-night spoke for some fruit for the country for my father against Christmas, and where should I do it but at the pretty woman's that used to stand at the door in Fenchurch Street, I having a mind to know her.' An astonishing number of the pretty women he met Pepys contrived somehow to kiss, and why he never got into trouble for it is more than I understand. The nearest approach to genuine resistance which he records was in St. Dunstan's Church, where, standing ' by a pretty modest maid,' he ' did labour,' he says, ' to take her by the hand and the body but she would not, but got further and further from me. And at last I could perceive her to take pins out of her pocket to prick me if I should touch her again ; which seeing I did forbear, and was glad I did spy her design.'

A great deal of this was quite disinterested admiration ; a pretty woman went to his head. But of course his wife took a more limited view. He struggled against it, and against all his other weaknesses, such as the theatre and strong drink ; made vows every year, and read them over every Lord's Day ; even priced his pet sins, and bought a poor-box, and fined himself for each delinquency. A kiss, it appears, cost him 12d., *after the first* : yet he ' did adventure upon a couple ' with pretty Mistress Margaret. Like most makers of vows he is a skilful evader. Hippocras, he decides, is a temperance drink. And why ? Because it is a mixed drink,—neither one thing nor another. And, of course, if one is *invited*

to the theatre, that is a very different thing
from deliberately going there. He was so
desperate once that he even lent the price of
his seat to a friend, so that his friend might
appear to be paying for him : but this, he
writes in penitence, was ' a fallacy to avoid
my vow with, but never to be more practised
I swear.' It was a great day for Pepys when
the first Drury Lane Theatre opened, and you
will never guess why. Because ' my oath
against going to plays do not oblige me against
this house, because it was not then in being ! '
Private vows, I am afraid, are things easily
got round. But they steadied him, and kept
his conscience lively.

Even so short a discourse as this would be
incomplete if I said nothing of Pepys's curi-
osity. It is endless. He notes always the first
time he either did or saw anything : the first
time he drank tea (' tee '), ' a China drink,'
or saw women on the stage ; the first time he
danced (' and did wonder at myself ') ; the
first time he used a razor (he had been content
with pumice stone before), or saw people
skating, or slept through a sermon, or took a
nap after dinner. He is the perfect sightseer,
for he can never be wholly disappointed.

Even if he does not like the thing, he is ' glad to have seen it once.' This lust of the eye makes him an admirable reporter. ' Here out of the window it was a most pleasant sight to see the City from one end to the other with a glory about it, so high was the light of the bonfires, and so thick round the City, and the bells rang everywhere.' It is the rejoicing for the return of King Charles, and what man of letters could have described it better? Pepys was as merry as anybody, drinking the King's health : ' if ever I was foxed it was now.' ' Up, and being ready I out to the goldsmith's, having not for some days been in the streets ; but now how few people I see, and those look-ing like people that had taken leave of the world.' Could the horror of the Plague of London be more tersely suggested? He saw the Great Fire of the following year, and has left us the best description of it : ' All over the Thames, with one's face in the wind, you were almost burned with a shower of fire-drops. . . . When we could endure no more upon the water, we to a little ale-house on the Bank-side, over against the Three Cranes, and there staid till it was dark almost, and saw the fire grow ; and, as it grew darker, appeared more and more, and in corners and upon steeples, and between churches and houses, as far as we could see up the hill of the City, in a most horrid malicious bloody flame, not like the fine flame of an ordinary fire. We staid till, it being darkish, we saw the fire as only one entire arch of fire from this to the other side the bridge, and in a bow up the hill for an arch of above a mile long : it made me weep to see it. The churches, houses, and all on fire and flaming at once ; and a horrid noise the flames made, and the cracking of houses at their ruin. So home with a sad heart.' Pepys was not idle during the fire ; he was never a mere spectator when there was work to be done. He toiled to save property, and his devotion may be measured by the state of his toilet, for he was unshaven for a week.

I leave him to your researches. He has given us in his Diary (which he closed too soon) a picture of his time among the most lifelike in history, and a portrait of a character as enduring as any of Shakespeare's, self-revealed.

November 17, 1926.

WALTON'S COMPLETE ANGLER

I THINK I may assume that *The Complete Angler* is to-day in very few hands. How indeed should it be otherwise ? So many books are in the world, all clamouring for our attention, and this is one of the quietest and least competitive. After an outburst of nineteenth century editions it has hidden itself again among the long grass.

I have heard people say that one must be a fisherman to enjoy it, but that is quite untrue. To enjoy the *Complete Angler* you need never have caught a fish, though if you have tried to do so you will enjoy it more. I am myself no sort of an angler, but the book has always been a refreshment to me. Fishermen, indeed, in spite of their deference to Father Izaak, have been its severest critics, for in many ways it is out-of-date both in fact and sentiment. Neither angling nor natural history has stood still, and few but schoolboys would now be satisfied with the baits of lob-worms and live maggots that contented Walton. The strength of the book, nevertheless, lies in this very archaism and simplicity. It is a refresh-

ment because it is *not* up-to-date, because the
England it describes, though unmistakably
England, is not the England of to-day. Walton's England is clean. The northern pro-
verb, ' Whar there 's muck there 's money,'
had not yet been invented, and Nature, on the
whole, still seemed cleverer than Man. The
rivers which Walton celebrates were unpol-
luted, and there were salmon in the Thames.
His milkmaids sing the ballads which we
collect, and in the milk they carry there is as
yet no water. No one is rich in Walton, and
no one is discontented, nor is there anything
faster in his pages than a trotting horse. This
sounds, you may say, extremely slow. It is,
thank God, and if speed is your object you
must turn to something else ; the *Complete
Angler* is not for you. Walton *teaches* peace and
quiet, for it is a mark of a good angler that he
is never noisy and never in a hurry. His book
is a lay-sermon on the unbustling nature of
happiness, preached out of doors under honey-
suckle hedges, and by the banks of streams.

Izaak Walton, when he published in 1653
the first edition of his *Angler*, was a retired
London merchant, an ex-linendraper in the
City, approaching the age of sixty. He was

a Stafford man originally, and having made a modest competence in Cornhill and Fleet Street, retired at fifty to enjoy the comforts of friendship and fishing. The two things go together, he tells us, for ' all anglers love one another.' His plan of life succeeded. He had forty years of leisure, wrote Lives of his friends which are the best biographies of the century, saw his *Angler* through five editions, and died at the age of ninety in equanimity and honour.

The full title of the book is a key to its character : *The Complete Angler, or The Contemplative Man's Recreation.* It is ' a picture,' he says, ' of my own disposition, especially in such days and times as I have laid aside business, and gone a-fishing with honest Nat. and R. Roe ' : adding, ' but they are gone, and with them most of my pleasant hours.' It is addressed not only to ' the honest angler ' (all good anglers are ' honest ' in Walton), but to any reader who is not ' too grave or too busy.' For that glum class of men Walton's pity is sincere : ' men that are taken to be grave, because nature hath made them of a sour complexion ; money-getting men . . . men that are condemned to be rich, and then always busy or discontented ; for these poor

rich men, we anglers pity them perfectly.'
' When the lawyer,' he says, ' is swallowed up
with business, and the statesman is preventing
or contriving plots, then we sit on cowslip-
banks, hear the birds sing, and possess ourselves in as much quietness as these silent
silver streams, which we now see glide so
quietly by us. Indeed . . . we may say of
angling as Dr. Butler said of strawberries—
" Doubtless God could have made a better
berry, but doubtless God never did " ; and so,
if I might be judge—" God never did make a
more calm, quiet, innocent recreation than
angling." ' So the good old man runs on.

The book opens on a fine May morning.
Three men, all lusty and hearty, are foot-
ing it out of London in the direction of Hert-
fordshire, just after sunrise. They greet each
other, and one, it appears, the senior, is going
fishing, another otter-hunting, and the third
to see some hawks. They discuss their respec-
tive sports, and there is a disposition in the
other two to laugh at fishermen as a simple
and unworldly class of men. Walton, in the
person of *Piscator*, makes no attempt to deny
this character ; indeed he proclaims it, and
reminds them that the same charge was made

against the first Christians, ' who were, as most
anglers are, quiet men, followers of peace.'
Why did Christ choose four simple fishermen
to be his disciples, and give them priority
among the Twelve ? Because ' he found that
the hearts of such men, by nature, were fitted
for contemplation and quietness.' This was
taking the matter a little high, and the
young men fall silent. The upshot is that
the otter-hunter has a ' call,' and becomes
his pupil.

The time covered is five days : a long week-
end, if it were conceivable that Izaak could
have fished on a Sunday. He is a benevolent
and loquacious instructor, but makes no
extravagant promises. He will show his pupil
how to fish, but ' the question is rather, whether
you will be capable of learning it ? for *angling
is somewhat like poetry, men are to be born so*.' The
angler-to-be must not only have an inquiring,
observing mind, but ' he must bring a large
measure of hope and patience, and a love and
propensity to the art itself.' [1] I will skip most

---

[1] On Angling as a school of Virtue, Sir John Hawkins,
Johnson's biographer and an early editor of Walton, is
equally emphatic. 'A man would think, now, that with
proper baits, good tackle in his pannier, and so much
science in his head, our angler would stand a pretty

of the directions about bait and flies, and the old-fashioned natural history. The heart of the book is in its picture of an ideal Old England and of the Old Angler himself. The birds sing through all his lessons, the hedges blossom, and the air is sweet with the English sun and the contentment of nature. I suppose the meeting with the milkmaid and her mother is the most famous of all his scenes. I must not tamper with it, but while you turn the pages let me recommend to you, also, the picture of the Otter Hunt, and the Gipsy Encampment, and the Jolly Beggars' Chorus. In the excitement of the hunt (which he is only persuaded to join because the otter is an enemy of fish) our contemplative Angler a little forgets his quietist principles. ' Let us be gone, let us make haste,' he cries, ' I long to be doing ; no reasonable hedge or ditch shall hold me.' The whole world seems out of doors and happy, and we pity, like Walton, the hard faces in the counting-house, which refuse to put away care.

good chance to catch fish ; but, alas ! those are little to the purpose, without the Christian virtues of *faith*, *hope* and *charity* ; and unless two at least of the *cardinal virtues* can be persuaded to go a-fishing, the angler may as well stay at home.'

When the day falls, or the sport is over, they are as happy indoors as out.   If any stranger should ask you where are the trim ale-houses of Old England, with their home-brewed tap, their smiling hostesses, and their lavendered sheets, tell him to look in Walton's *Angler*, and while he is about it, see our fishermen at supper in Trout Hall—see them eat, and hear them sing.   For everyone can sing in Walton, and read his part at sight.   They draw cuts and the lot falls on Coridon, a neighbouring farmer ; he wets his whistle and begins :

> Oh the sweet contentment
> The countryman doth find !
> *Heigh trolie lollie loe,*
> *Heigh trolie lollie lee,*
> That quiet contemplation
> Possesseth all my mind :
> *Then, care away,*
> *And wend along with me.*
>
> For courts are full of flattery,
> As hath too oft been tried ;
> *Heigh trolie lollie loe, etc.*
> The city full of wantonness,
> And both are full of pride,
> *Then, care away,*
> *And wend along with me.*
>
> But oh ! the honest countryman
> Speaks truly from his heart ;
> *Heigh trolie lollie loe, etc.*

His pride is in his tillage,
His horses and his cart,
Then, care away,
And wend along with me.

*   *   *   *

This is not half the happiness
The countryman enjoys ;
Heigh trolie lollie loe, etc.,
Though others think they have as
much,
Yet he that says so, lies :
Then, come away,
Turn countryman with me.

' Well sung, Coridon ! ', cries *Piscator*, ' this song was sung with mettle ; it was choicely fitted to the occasion ; I shall love you for it as long as I know you. I would you were a brother of the angle ; for a companion that is cheerful, and free from swearing and scurrilous discourse, is worth gold.'

No wonder that Charles Lamb (though no angler) fell in love with the book. ' It would sweeten a man's temper at any time to read it,' he says, ' and Christianize every discordant passion.' He recommended it, like Dr. Johnson,[1] to young men, and more especially

---

[1] Johnson had a liking for the book. It seems not to be generally known that he was the instigator of the Rev. Moses Browne's edition of the *Angler* (1750), which started a Walton revival.

to the highly strung whose wits needed air-
ing. ' I shall expect you,' he writes to one
of these, ' to bring me a brimful account of
the pleasure which Walton has given you,
when you come to Town. . . . The delightful innocence and healthfulness of the Angler's
mind will have blown upon yours like a Zephyr.
Don't you already feel your spirit *filled* with the
scenes ?—the banks of rivers—the cowslip beds
—the pastoral scenes—the neat alehouses—and
hostesses and milkmaids . . .? Are not the
eating and drinking joys painted to the life ?
Do they not inspire you with an immortal
hunger ? Are not you ambitious of being
made an Angler ? . . . The *Complete Angler* is
the only Treatise written in Dialogues that is
worth a halfpenny. Many elegant dialogues
have been written . . . but in all of them the
Interlocutors are merely abstract arguments
personify'd ; not living dramatic characters,
as in Walton, where *everything* is *alive* ; the
fishes are absolutely *charactered* ; and birds
and animals are as interesting as men and
women.'

The old anglers were all-round craftsmen.
Most modern anglers get their flies at a shop ;
these others made their flies, and plundered the

feathered world to do it.   The modern angler, as a rule, considers his work done when he has caught his fish ; but the old anglers were as learned in the cooking as in the catching of it. Walton's directions for cooking chub, it has been truly said, read 'like a chapter in Leviticus.' His lordly recipe for pike, the fresh water tyrant, abounds in admonitions which would be the despair of the paltry house-keeping of modern times. This was a private recipe ; it takes two pages, and was 'very choice.' 'This dish of meat,' he says, 'is too good for any but anglers, or very honest men ; and I trust you will prove both ; and therefore I have trusted you with this secret.'

The modern angler, making his first acquaintance with Walton, is surprised, and sometimes a little shocked, to discover that he was habitually a mere fisher with bait. It was the way of his time. Though excellent fly-fishers existed, the vast majority were simple bottom-fishers like Walton. Shakespeare, a Warwickshire sportsman, seems to have been familiar with no other method, and had never known the pleasure of fishing fine and far off in a clear stream. Walton's directions for fly-fishing are confessedly at second-hand, though he had fished in Dovedale with an expert, his friend and disciple Charles Cotton, and had a bedroom there waiting for him, at Beresford in the Peak,—' my father Walton's chamber,'—whenever he cared to occupy it, and a fishing-house to sit in on the banks of the Dove, with his own and Cotton's initials lovingly entwined over the lintel. (He promises a visit in his eighty-third year, ' though I be more than a hundred miles from you.') Walton is never a pretender. As Scott remarked, he knew his sphere, and ' we no more expect him to soar beyond it, and to kill, for example, a salmon of twenty pounds weight with a single hair, than we would look to see his brother linen-draper, John Gilpin, leading a charge of hussars.' Yet this ' London shopkeeper dapping for chubs ' acquired in his lifetime the veneration due to a philosopher, and remains to this day the sentimental Father of all his tribe.

' I am not of a cruel nature,' says Walton. ' I love to kill nothing but fish.' This sentence, which only extreme bean-eaters will take amiss, leads me to the one blot in the old man's book : a certain paragraph on live-bait,

which gave Byron, who disliked angling, a
chance to strike our friend. One could have
told that Byron would dislike fishing. It is
not a pastime for revolutionaries and home-
breakers ; I wish it were. If a taste for
angling could be universally diffused, we
should have no more agitations. Byron de-
nounces angling, and charges Walton with
cruelty :

> And angling, too, that solitary vice,
> Whatever Izaak Walton sings or says,
> The quaint old cruel coxcomb, in his gullet,
> Should have a hook, and a small trout to
>   pull it.

Why all this acrimony ?   Because of Walton's
directions for fitting a live frog to a hook when
you are fishing for pike. It had apparently
never occurred to him that this was cruel,—
nor probably to any one else at that time.
Indeed he is almost comically earnest that
you should not hurt the poor creature, at the
very moment when he is advising you how to
dissect and impale it.   Here are his directions
—partly copied, it has been urged, from an
earlier treatise. ' Put your hook into his
mouth, which you may easily do from the

middle of April till August; and then the frog's mouth grows up, and he continues so for at least six months without eating, but is sustained, none but He whose Name is Wonderful knows how : I say, put your hook . . . through his mouth, and out at his gills, and then with a fine needle and silk sew the upper part of his leg with only one stitch, to the arming-wire of your hook, or tie the frog's leg above the upper joint to the armed wire ; and in so doing, use him as though you loved him, that is, harm him as little as you may possibly, so that he may live the longer.' I confess I cannot cope with the strains of thought in this remarkable sentence. ' Good kind old soul was Walton,' cries a judicious admirer, ' but could you have trusted him with a baby, for instance, if some one had told him that a bit of baby was a capital bait for barbel ? ' Such are the frailties of enthusiasm in even the gentlest minds !

The *Complete Angler* was at one time a special favourite of publishers, and for other than merely commercial reasons. They had a habit, in that profession, of being anglers as well. Most of the numerous editions of the first half of the nineteenth century, from

Bagster's (1808) to Bohn's (1856), show evidence of this double interest and care. In Walton's time, if we may judge from his pages, angling seems to have been the favourite pastime of churchmen and poets. His book is sprinkled with pious commemorations of them, as with holy water (for it was a penalty of his great age that he outlived so many) : ' an excellent angler,' he will say, ' and now with God.' One clerical angler whom he names with honour, Dr. Nowell, Dean of St. Paul's, outstepped him in years, and is otherwise notable. He had his picture drawn, with his bible before him and his fishing-tackle round him, to typify the happy duality of his interests ; and he made a surprising discovery the effects of which we still enjoy. It is recorded of him that ' leaving a *Bottle of Ale* (when fishing) in the *Grass*, he found it some days after, no *Bottle*, but a *Gun*, such the sound at the opening thereof : And this is believed (casualty is *Mother* of more *Inventions* than *Industry*) the Original of *bottled Ale* in England ! '

But I have run out my time. I will leave you as Walton leaves the reader in his Preface—wishing you, what in this island is never hard to come by, ' a rainy evening ' to read his book in, and praying, if you be ' an honest angler,' that ' the east wind may never blow when you go a-fishing.'

November 24, 1926.

IF there are in my audience any confirmed lovers of this book, any life-long Shandeans, any to whom the parlour at Shandy Hall, with its conversational hearth and its creaking door-hinge, and the ever-memorable bowling green across the way, are as familiar as the prospect from their own windows,—if there are any such now listening, I would ask them to consider whether it might not be advisable to abandon me at the outset, and devote themselves instead to interpreting (shall I say?) some of the asterisks of that immortal work, or to filling up the blank pages of chapter cxcviii. You know the place : it is the unwritten catalogue of the Widow Wadman's charms. 'Paint her to your own mind,' says Sterne,—for he knew his business too well to do it himself,—' as like your mistress as you can,—as unlike your wife as your conscience will let you,—'tis all one to me.' And I may add, to me also. While you are thus occupied, and safely remounted on the Shandean hobby-horse, I can proceed with my affair. My affair is not with you, but with the uninitiated :

with those to whom Uncle Toby, even, and
Corporal Trim are no more than names.

*The Life and Opinions of Tristram Shandy,
Gentleman*—to give the book its full title—came
out in parts, as they were written, between
the years 1760 and 1767, and took not only
London but the continent of Europe by storm.
Its author, Laurence Sterne, was a Yorkshire
clergyman of no particular note—until that
moment. It was his first real book, and he
was nearing fifty when he began to print it.
It has all the marks of such an origin ; the
whole man, bottled and effervescing, is in it.
He had repressed himself so long. It is bursting with confidences about everything under
the sun, all that he had thought and felt and
suffered and enjoyed. The time was come
when he must either explode or express himself, and being a man of genius he jumped the
alternative, and did both. He was ailing when
he wrote most of it, and died the year after it
was finished. But he had eight years of fame
and lionising, which he enormously enjoyed,
to make up for his thirty years' obscurity.

Tristram Shandy is not an easy book to describe : the puzzle is, where to begin. I will
be frank, also, and confess that though it has

something for everybody, it is not, and never can be, everybody's book. There are things in it which give offence, for which Sterne needs forgiveness, and he does not always get it. On the other hand, I know excellent and exemplary people who seldom travel without a copy of *Tristram*. The book is written, also, in a very odd and eccentric manner, like no other book, probably, that you have ever met : full of asterisks and blank spaces, and now and then a whole blank page to set you staring— with the Dedication in chapter viii, and the Preface, will you believe it, in chapter lxiv— all topsy-turvy, higgledy-piggledy—*apparently* ; though, in fact, the most cunning and exquisite art is at work all the while, contriving, suggesting, and drawing out before us that odd household of humourists, who are the core and centre of the book, the great family of SHANDY.

As the Shandy family did nothing like any other family, it is fitting that Tristram, its descendant and historian, should be unlike all other authors. His father had predicted this singularity, in words which Sterne appropriates to himself. ' My uncle Toby well remembered, upon his observing a most unaccountable obliquity (as he called it) in my manner of setting up my top ; and justifying the principles upon which I had done it,—the old gentleman shook his head, and in a tone more expressive by half of sorrow than reproach, he said his heart all along foreboded, and he saw it verified in this, and from a thousand other observations he had made upon me, that I should neither think nor act like any other man's child.' Sterne delights in digressions, flying off, as he puts it, ' according as the fly stings,' and leaving his readers standing. He hobnobs and has little dialogues with them. ' Shut the door,' he will say,—' I have something confidential to tell you.' Or he imagines interruptions. ' What did you say, Madam ? ', he will ask. ' No, Madam, you are wrong.' Or,—' Lay down the book, and I will allow you half a day,' to guess how it was. He prides himself on keeping his readers guessing, and ' in this, Sir,' he says, ' I am of so nice and singular a humour, that if I thought you was able to form the least judgment, or probable conjecture to yourself of what was to come in the next page,—I would tear it out of the book.'

This whimsical suspense is kept up throughout. He believed that good writing—' as you may be sure I think mine is '—is only a different name for conversation. As it is wrong when one is in company to do all the talking, so it is wrong for an author to do all the thinking. ' The truest respect which you can pay to the reader's understanding is to halve the matter amicably, and leave him something to imagine in his turn, as well as yourself.' ' For my own part,' he goes on, ' I am eternally paying him compliments of this kind, and do all that lies in my power to keep his imagination as busy as my own. *'Tis his turn now!* ' Here is a fair offer, and an offer which few authors are in a position to make. More than anything else, it is this partnership of effort which makes *Tristram Shandy* the exciting book it is. You can put the book down. You can throw it to the farthest corner of the room— the thing has been done. But you cannot read it and remain half awake.

Sterne is a great craftsman, and is proud of his skill. Watch me !, he says. The machinery of *Tristram* he holds to be ' a species by itself,' and certainly it would be hard to parallel. He maintains throughout the book two contrary and simultaneous motions : one quietly progressive, the other madcap and tangential, — here and everywhere. I do openly confess, he says, that I ' fly off from what I am about, as far, and as often too, as any writer in Great Britain,—yet I constantly take care to order affairs so, that my main business does not stand still in my absence. I was just going, for example, to have given you the great outlines of my uncle Toby's most whimsical character ;—when my aunt Dinah and the coachman came across us, and led us a vagary . . . : notwithstanding all this, you perceive the drawing of my uncle Toby's character went on gently all the time.' It is perfectly true ; it does.

Sterne's one declared enemy is Gravity, False Gravity : ' great wigs, and grave faces, and other implements of deceit.' He had suffered from them, no doubt, in the diocese of York. He was of Yorick's opinion, that Gravity is commonly a scoundrel, and of the most dangerous kind, because a sly one : ' 't was a taught trick, to gain credit of the world.' There is an ancient conspiracy of the solemn doltheads of all countries to discredit men of wit. Trust, they seem to say, us heavy dull men, for wit can never mislead us. Against this conspiracy Sterne takes up our cause. 'Do—pull of your beards,' he cries to these pretenders, the hypocritical long faces of the world. 'Unless this vile cough kills me in the mean time ',—it did kill him, it was killing him then,—'I 'll have another pluck at your beards.' His recipe was Shandeism: for 'true Shandeism, think what you will against it, opens the heart and lungs . . . , forces the blood and other vital liquids of the body to run freely through their channels, and makes the wheel of life run long and cheerfully round.'

I have given you some taste of the Shandean philosophy. It remains to introduce the Shandy family. Walter, the head of the house, is a retired London merchant with cranks and crotchets about everything, a reader of out-of-the-way books and a propounder of chains of reasoning. My uncle Toby, his younger brother, is a veteran of King William's wars against the French, now retired, with his wound, his maps, and his faithful man-servant Corporal Trim, to the mock warfare of his bowling green. Mrs. Shandy is Walter's wife. She says little and does much, and agrees implicitly with her husband in all unessential matters. His theories, which might have alarmed another woman, leave her quite unmoved, partly because she does not understand them, but chiefly because she is confident that the laws of nature can defend themselves. Tristram, her son, is rather a symbol than a character, and is chiefly occupied in being born. There is also Yorick the parson, in whose delicate and tender portrait much of Sterne is concealed ('his character was—he loved a jest in his heart') ; Dr. Slop the physician, a sturdy personage whom Sterne might have developed if he had had room ; Obadiah the man, and Susannah the maid of spirit ; and over the way, planning the downfall of Toby's celibacy, the Widow Wadman and her maid Bridget.

Now the odd and entertaining thing about this Shandy household,—I mean the parlour end of it,—and by the easy device of leaving the parlour door a quarter open, there was little went on in the parlour that was not presently rehearsed in the kitchen,—I say the odd thing about them was, that though they dearly loved each other, and had hearts of gold, not one of the family understood any other. Their dialogues are one long cross-

purpose ; and with every appearance of being
listened to, not one of them, in fact, is really
listened to at all. Uncle Toby was saved by
Trim, who shared his sole hobby of mimic
warfare and fortification. Mrs. Shandy was
saved by understanding nothing of what was
said, and having plenty to do in regions where
logic and demi-culverins did not count. The
really desolate figure, the thwarted hero of
this tragi-comedy, is Walter Shandy, on whom
it is gradually forced that the wife of his bosom,
and the brother whom he loves, try as they may,
understand not one essential of any theory he
may broach. ' My uncle Toby would give my
father all possible fair play in this attempt ;
and with infinite patience would sit smoking
his pipe for whole hours together, whilst my
father was practising upon his head.' It was
to no purpose. A glance would wound his
heart, but uncle Toby's head defied incision.
Sterne, it has been remarked, had he been
bitter, might have made a satire out of all this
on the futility and incompetence of the human
race. He has presented us, instead, with a
picture of a family which by the queerest
routes, from pure innocence and goodness of
heart, conquers all misunderstandings, and

achieves the blundering felicity of human happiness.

Uncle Toby, as we have seen, had his own preoccupations. But Mrs. Shandy had grown up with her husband's theories, and continued to ignore them and to love him not a whit the less. ' Cursed luck ! ', growled her husband, after one of his failures, ' for a man to be master of one of the finest chains of reasoning in nature,—and have a wife at the same time with such a headpiece, that he cannot hang up a single inference within side of it, to save his soul from destruction.' If she had only asked a question, he would have been enchanted to answer her. ' It was a consuming vexation to my father that my mother never asked the meaning of a thing she did not understand. That she is not a woman of science, my father would say, is her misfortune ; but she might ask a question. My mother never did. In short, she went out of the world, at last, not knowing whether it *turned round*, or *stood still*. My father had officiously told her above a thousand times which way it was ;— but she always forgot.'

My uncle Toby is the kindest and simplest nature in the world, and so lovingly drawn that I cannot, in these few moments, do justice to him, or to the lines and colours of his creator. It is said of him by Sterne, in a story which sounds like a memory of his own boyhood,—for Sterne was a soldier's son and had known many soldier worthies,—that he, Captain Shandy, of Leven's Brigade, the stout veteran of the famous siege of Namur, could literally not bring himself, hostilities apart, to hurt any living thing. ' All was mixed up so kindly within him ; my uncle Toby had scarce a heart to retaliate upon a fly.—Go,—says he one day at dinner, to an overgrown one, which had buzzed about his nose, and tormented him cruelly all dinner-time,—and which, after infinite attempts, he had caught at last as it flew by him ;—I 'll not hurt thee, says my uncle Toby, rising from his chair, and going across the room, with the fly in his hand.—I 'll not hurt a hair of thy head :—Go, says he, lifting up the sash, and opening his hand as he spoke, to let it escape ;—go, poor devil, get thee gone, why should I hurt thee ?—This world surely is wide enough to hold both thee and me.'

I wish I could read to you the fine scene, in chapter cxxxiii, of those two great children, uncle Toby and his man Trim, at work among their mimic engines on what was once a bowling green, reducing daily by siege, in strict accordance with the Flanders bulletin, models of the cities which the Allied Armies were then beleaguering. It was unfair to disturb their boyish and harmless pleasures by an irruption of the Sex. I have something in my eye, said the Widow Wadman, issuing through the wicket-gate, and approaching Captain Shandy's sentry-box. ' Do look into it :—it is not in the white.' Uncle Toby looked. ' Now of all the eyes which ever were created ;—from your own, Madam, up to those of Venus herself . . . ,— there never was an eye of them all so fitted to rob my uncle Toby of his repose, as the very eye at which he was looking ;—it was not, Madam, a rolling eye,—a romping,—or a wanton one ;—nor was it an eye sparkling, petulant, or imperious,—of high claims and terrifying exactions, which would have curdled at once that milk of human nature, of which my uncle Toby was made up ;—but 't was an eye full of gentle salutations,—and soft responses,—speaking,—not like the trumpet-stop of some ill-made organ, in which many an eye I talk to holds coarse converse, but whispering

soft,—like the last low accents of an expiring
saint,—" How can you live comfortless, Captain Shandy, and alone, without a bosom to
lean your head on,—or trust your cares to ? "
It was an eye——But I shall be in love with it
myself, if I say another word about it.—It did
my uncle Toby's business.'   It did, effectually ;
and we are doubtful whether to be amused or
sorry.

Tristram Shandy is enriched with unexpected
charming stories, and vignettes of scenes and
persons, thrown in by its author as a kind of
bonus or reward.   There is the tale—a little
laboured, now, we think it, but still touching
—of the poor lieutenant, Le Fever.   And in a
slighter style, in which no one can compete
with him, the picture of the pretty Janatone,
the inn-keeper's daughter at Montreuil : ' a
slut ! in running them over within these five
minutes that I have stood looking at her, she
has let fall at least a dozen loops in a white
thread stocking.—Yes, yes,—I see, you cunning
gipsy !—'t is long and taper,—you need not
pin it to your knee ;—and that 't is your own,—
and fits you exactly.'   There is the story of
Nanette (' A sun-burnt daughter of Labour
rose up from the group to meet me——'), and

how they danced together, torn petticoat and all, under the trees on the Nismes road. But the best is the adventure at Lyons. I was leaving my inn, he says, when I was stopped at the gate.

'T was by a poor ass, who had just turned in with a couple of large panniers upon his back, to collect eleemosynary turnip-tops and cabbage-leaves ; and stood dubious with his two fore-feet on the inside of the threshold, and with his two hinder-feet towards the street, as not know-ing very well whether he was to go in or no.

Now 't is an animal (be in what hurry I may) I cannot bear to strike ;—there is a patient endurance of sufferings, wrote so unaffectedly in his looks and carriage . . . ,—I have ever something civil to say to him on my part ; and as one word begets another . . . I generally fall into conversation with him ; and surely never is my imagination so busy as in framing his responses from the etchings of his counten-ance,—and where those carry me not deep enough,—in flying from my own heart into his, and seeing what is natural for an ass to think. . . . With an ass, I can commune for ever.

— Come, Honesty ! said I, . . . art thou for coming in, or going out ?

— The ass twisted his head round, to look up the street.

— Well, replied I, we 'll wait a minute for thy driver.

— He turned his head thoughtful about, and looked wistfully the opposite way.

I understand thee perfectly, answered I ;—if thou takest a wrong step in this affair, he will cudgel thee to death. . . .

He was eating the stem of an artichoke as this discourse went on, and, in the little peevish contentions of nature betwixt hunger and un-savouriness, had dropped it out of his mouth half a dozen times, and picked it up again.— God help thee, Jack ! said I, thou hast a bitter breakfast on 't,—and many a bitter day's labour, —and many a bitter blow, I fear, for its wages !— And now thy mouth, if one knew the truth of it, is as bitter, I dare say, as soot—(for he had cast aside the stem), and thou hast not a friend in the world, perhaps, that will give thee a macaroon. —In saying this, I pulled out a paper of 'em, which I had just purchased, and gave him one. . . .

When the ass had eaten his macaroon, I pressed him to come in ;—the poor beast was heavy loaded,—his legs seemed to tremble under him,—he hung rather backwards ; and, as I pulled at his halter, it broke short in my hand.—He looked up pensive in my face— ' Don't thrash me with it ;—but, if you will, you may.'—If I do, said I, I 'll be d——d.

The word was but one half of it pronounced . . . when a person coming in, let fall a thundering bastinado upon the poor devil's crupper.

The conversation ceased, and the world again took control. But can you blame me that I have found it irresistible ? And that I have chosen it, and indeed forced it upon you, as the last delicacy of our Shandean repast? The qualities of Sterne and the condiments of Shandeism are not easily defined. ('Who are you?' said he. 'Don't puzzle me,' said I.) But some of the best of both are in this scene.

December 15, 1926.

BOSWELL'S LIFE OF JOHNSON

IT is late in the day to be advancing the merits of Boswell's *Life of Johnson*, and pressing its claims as a companionable book. Probably no English publication of the last hundred and thirty years has made more friends or kept them longer. Its votaries are of all ages and both sexes, and their number, which has always been large, seems to be constantly increasing. It has increased very notably in the last twenty years. There is something in the character of Johnson, and in Boswell's portrait of him, which evidently appeals with peculiar force to the age in which we are now living. I suppose it is partly a great weariness of make-believe that has directed so many eyes upon him, and is now replacing the spent wind of Victorian idealism with his Georgian robustness and his majestic common sense. We are a somewhat disillusioned generation. The rainbow promises of our fathers have not been kept, and we turn with relief to this sworn enemy of cant, who never pretended even to himself that life can yield more than we are willing to put into it, or that Utopia can be reached by exhalations of the breath. 'When a butcher tells you that his heart bleeds for his country, he has in fact no uneasy feeling.'

We are conscious, also—which is another reason—standing among the scientific wonders of our day, that while we have gained in power, we have lost in art, and most notably, perhaps, in the chief art of all. Human power is enormous, but in the chaos of new contrivances we have somehow contrived to lose the art of living. Now this, as it happens, is precisely the art which the eighteenth century and Johnson have to teach us. It is an art of dignity, simplicity, and quiet, and by a kind of homing instinct we are returning to it.

I said that the devotees of Boswell's *Johnson* are of both sexes and of all ages. Yet it is a man's book, and its talk is men's talk. It is humorous, but also profoundly rational, and hardly anything in it could have been said by a woman, or, for that matter, by a lover or a child. Children appear only as a topic, to have their education settled, and women, for the most part, as a social problem. The affair of love, on the rare occasions when it is mentioned, is treated either as a theme for poets, or as an occasion for prudence. To some extent this is a result of the Boswellian method. The Johnson who played the elephant with the little Thrales,—who, if he had had ' no duties, and no reference to futurity,' would have spent his life ' in driving briskly in a post-chaise with a pretty woman ',—the Johnson who had ' more fun, and comical humour, and love of nonsense about him ' than almost anybody Fanny Burney ever saw, is sparsely represented in Boswell's pages. No man more than Johnson enjoyed the society of the tea-table, or set a higher value on the company of elegant, sensible, and vivacious women. The happiest time of his life, he told Mrs. Thrale, was when he spent ' one whole evening ' talking with Molly Aston—' the loveliest creature I ever saw,' and a wit and a scholar besides. ' That indeed, was not happiness, it was rapture ; but the thoughts of it sweetened the whole year.' This side of Johnson was not to be ignored, but it made Boswell jealous and uneasy. He had neither eyes nor ears for the ladies when Johnson was in the room, and seems almost to have grudged his hero's gallantry because it offered so little to the reporter. This was not, I must add, because Boswell was unsusceptible of female charm. ' I got into a fly at Buckden,' he writes to a friend, ' and had a very good journey. An agreeable young widow nursed me and supported my lame foot on her knee. Am I not fortunate in having something about me that interests most people at first sight in my favour ? ' This was in a fly, when he was off duty. In Johnson's company his business was with Johnson, and Johnson, he thought, was more Johnsonian among men. I have no doubt that he was right. But there was a great deal of Johnson.

The book, then, is masculine, though not forbiddingly so. I first met it as a schoolboy, and remember still the almost magical impression of it. Here, by turning a few pages, I found myself admitted not only to a larger world, but actually to a Club, and, as I was to verify later, the best Club in literature. My case is not uncommon. The late Sir Leslie Stephen declared, at the close of a life devoted to authorship and letters, that his enjoyment of books had begun and ended with Boswell's *Life of Johnson.*

Though it suits all ages, it is a book, I fancy, best appreciated in the middle years, and by

those who have had to fight for their experience, who have not found life easy, and who are
still in the battle.   Intelligence is not enough,
even superior intelligence, as Macaulay proved.
No admirer of this book has more disastrously
misunderstood it.   To understand Johnson it
is necessary to have lived and to have thought
about life, for life was his trade.   He was
notoriously a great bookman, ' the literary
Colossus of his age,' but as a guide to his conversation this character is misleading.   The
book he read most diligently was ' the great
book of mankind,' and by this he tried all
others.   His talk is quite unbookish.   It is
exercised by preference on the topics of daily
life, and has a pungency and decision hardly
ever to be met with except in the occasional
utterances of strong uneducated minds.   This
unspoiled power Johnson habitually employed,
and its product, fortified by literature, is
unique.   He does easily and triumphantly
what few do even well : he cross-examines
life.   Continued from day to day, and from
month to month, it is the greatest Trial
Scene in history, and Boswell is its inspired
recorder.

Johnson's own life, till he neared sixty, was

a long and proud struggle against poverty,
melancholy, and disease, and the courage as
well as the kindliness of his wisdom was derived
from that struggle. If literature is a ladder
he started fair, for he began at the bottom rung.
'I can hardly tell,' he said, 'who was my
grandfather.' All the untender mercies which
that age held out to authors he had experi-
enced. He had starved, and walked the streets.
He had known the Garret, the Patron, and the
Jail. 'Seven years, my Lord, have now past
since I waited in your outward rooms, or was
repulsed from your door . . .' Need I go
on ? Or has that great music of the Letter to
Lord Chesterfield still some ears to capture ?
It is the voice of all the poor and proud men in
the world. Johnson was a famous satirist in
his younger days, and with more reason than
most satirists can show. But he early gave up
complaining, and found that we grow more
good-humoured as we grow older. He was
content to startle his company with such
occasional remarks as this : 'He that sees
before him to a third dinner has a large prospect.' His mind was never soured, but
remained humorous, whimsical, and playful.
Experience had made him severe with him-

self, but tolerant of frailty in others. His tenderness to the outcast, in 'a world bursting with sin and sorrow,' is as characteristic of the man as his Toryism and love of argument.

The public purse of this country was never better employed than when it procured for Johnson, by means of a modest pension, the opportunity of cultivating the art of life in comfort. The greater part of his last twenty years was devoted to talk and friendship. They are the years which Boswell principally records, when Johnson lay, after the storms of life, like a man-of-war in harbour receiving visitors. Had this harbourage been denied we should still have heard great echoes of him, but the chances are that he would have been too busy to be Boswellized. We should have lost, it is probable, Boswell's *Life*, and by losing that should have lost, not Samuel Johnson, but the best picture in all literature of a living great man.

'You have made them all talk Johnson,' said a friend to Boswell in 1791, when the *Life* was in its first edition. 'Yes,' said Boswell, 'I have *Johnsonized* the land ; and I trust they will not only *talk*, but *think* Johnson.' To 'talk Johnson' now would be absurd, though after Shakespeare no dead Englishman is oftener quoted. But to 'think Johnson' can never be obsolete. It is one of the distinctions of Boswell, and a sign of his superiority of mind, that he so clearly saw this. To 'think Johnson' is, very simply, to have a habit of truth. It is in all situations to insist on the facts, and to face them when found. It is to refuse, at whatever cost, to make life seem better than it is. It is to 'clear the mind of cant.' It is to practise true statement not only in the most important things, but in the least. No one can have lived long who thinks this habit common. No one has tried it who thinks it easy. Sir Joshua Reynolds noted that all who were of Johnson's 'school'—it is Sir Joshua's own word—were 'distinguished for a love of truth and accuracy, which they would not have possessed in the same degree if they had not been acquainted with him.' To this 'school,' as to its master and its famous company of graduates, Boswell's *Life* is the official guide, and I can imagine no more entertaining 'Introduction to Veracity.' Shall we be Johnson's 'scholars'—I risk the question— and put up at his academy? In a world humming with lies, and what is still more dangerous, a world honeycombed with inaccuracy, I appeal for entrants to a ' school ' which is none too well filled.

December 1, 1926.

COWPER'S LETTERS

WE are all letter-writers and receivers of letters, and have a personal interest, therefore, in the art. If there *is* an art of letter-writing, which may be doubted. There are formulae, it is true, for letters of ceremony or business, and it is of the nature of a formula that it can be learnt. But no acceptable equation has yet been discovered for a letter to a friend. In this kind of writing—and nearly all the best letters have had a friend for their destination—the wisest instructor is the heart. What, for example, is the formula for this ? ' I thank you, my dear,' writes Cowper to his cousin Lady Hesketh, ' for the snip of cloth commonly called a pattern. I have two coats, and but one back. If at any time hereafter I should find myself possessed of fewer coats or more backs, it will be of use to me.' This is not cleverness ; anybody can be clever. It is humour bred upon affection.

Take another occasion—ordinary enough—though it was a great event to Cowper. This same cousin was coming to see him, with her own horses and carriage, and he was afraid that she would take the wrong turn. So he arranged that she should be met at the critical corner by his gardener Kitchener, called Kitch for short. 'I shall set him on horseback,' he says, 'and order him to the "Swan" at Newport, there to await your arrival. . . . The first man, therefore, you shall see in a blue coat, with white buttons, in the famous town of Newport, cry "Kitch!" He will immediately answer, "My Lady!", and from that moment you are sure not to be lost.' There is nothing remarkable about this except that it is perfect letter-writing. The writer is in complete understanding with his correspondent, and his mind is easy and at play.

The letters of William Cowper are among the best in the language, but he would have repudiated the suggestion that they are works of art. His poems—yes ; these he would labour at, and revise endlessly. But what place is there for art in letters to one's friends ? All such letters, he says, should be ' of the true helter-skelter kind.' Most of his own letters were written out of mere affection, without his knowing when he began what he intended to say, or whether he had anything to say at all. They are totally unpremeditated, and flow from him like talk.

The truth is, of course, that letter-writing is like conversation : a social thing. It takes *two* to make a good letter. The first article in the equipment of a letter-writer is not a turn for phrases, but a friend ; and the first personal requisite is the generosity to value friendship. If these are available no obstacle need be apprehended ; you have only to draw your chair in, dip your pen, and be honestly yourself. If either of these requisites is absent no ability or skill can possibly make up for them. It is not the clever letters that have lasted—the letters written for admiration and to be handed about. The best letters have always been private letters, addressed, like Cowper's, to the smallest possible audience, an audience of one. How highly he valued this privacy is evident from his behaviour when he discovered that it was being broken, that his letters were being shown and praised. ' Your mother communicated to me the satisfaction you expressed in my correspondence, that you thought me entertaining, and clever, and so forth. Now you must know I love praise dearly, especially from the judicious, and those who have so much deli-

cacy themselves as not to offend mine in
giving it. But then, I found this consequence
attending, or likely to attend, the eulogium
you bestowed—if my friend thought me witty
before, he shall think me ten times more witty
hereafter—where I joked once, I will joke five
times, and, for one sensible remark, I will send
him a dozen. Now this foolish vanity would
have spoiled me quite, and would have made
me as disgusting a letter-writer as Pope, who
seems to have thought that unless a sentence
was well-turned, and every period pointed
with some conceit, it was not worth the
carriage. Accordingly he is to me, except in
a very few instances, the most disagreeable
maker of epistles that ever I met with. I
was willing, therefore, to wait till the impression
your commendation had made upon the
foolish part of me was worn off, that I might
scribble away as usual, and write my uppermost thoughts, and those only.' That his
letters have survived, and that the English
public is privileged to read them—that we can
still look over Lady Hesketh's shoulder at mail-
time—this is a matter for much thankfulness,
but it was none of Cowper's doing. He would
rather, I fancy, that they had been burned as

soon as read. They had conveyed their message.

It was the tragedy of Cowper's life that only his uppermost thoughts, as he calls them, would bear writing. Let me briefly say what that life was. It will help me to place my subject if I remind you that Cowper died in 1800, at the age of sixty-eight, and that the great majority of his letters belong to the last twenty years of his life. When he first comes before us as a correspondent he appears as a person of no particular consequence, living in a kind of enforced retirement, on an allowance from his relatives, with some religious friends in the valley of the Ouse,—first at Huntingdon, and then, for many years, at Olney in North Buckinghamshire. He is a man, it appears further, with no profession, though he had been bred to the law ; idle, therefore, except for employments of his own or his friends' invention ; and (which explains all the rest) haunted by the terrors of a religious delusion. That his birth and breeding had been gentle we could tell even if we did not know, and there escape from him signs and reminiscences of a cheerful and vivacious youth. Vivacity, indeed, is natural to him, and twinkles merrily out of his fog and all but his blackest apprehensions. He has an instinctive pleasure in living and growing things, in trees and flowers and birds and beasts, and delights no less in the delicate niceties of indoor life : is even a little dandyish on his good days, spending more on shoe-buckles than on books. Though shy and retiring, he is devoted to the society of a few selected friends.

The story has been often told. He had had a nervous breakdown in his thirty-second year, when he was a barrister in the Middle Temple, and had fallen into the despairing belief, which never wholly left him, that he alone of men, he, in fact, the most innocent of men, was excluded for ever from the mercy of Christ and damned beyond redemption. He was shut up for a time, but the cloud lifted, and he withdrew from public duties and from the contagion, as he regarded it, of London, to the country retirement which he was never to leave. Fortunately he had always friends, and at every turn and crisis of his life Providence, which otherwise had treated him so ill, raised up devoted women to cheer and, very literally, to inspire him. The cloud returned upon him more than once and in the end overwhelmed him, but out of his last twenty years he stole cheerfulness and activity enough to become the most popular poet of his day, and, though he thought little of that, the best letter-writer also. The record of these years is in his letters, and his letters would be worth reading, if for no other reason, merely to see what a man can do with his life against such odds.

He was approaching fifty when the change occurred which was to make him a famous poet, and to make letter-writing one of his principal pleasures. After years of experiment he had brought at last to perfection his peculiar art of living : the art of being perpetually occupied (for he dare not be idle), of making trifles (since real business was denied him) a shield against insanity. It was a game played against Despair, and with such a smiling courage and finesse, with such childlike but successful stratagem, as can hardly be paralleled in any other life. The little world of the letters, the tame hares he kept, his linnet and his robins, his gardening and carpentry, the unadventurous walks and visits, and all the petty annals of a small house and garden in a secluded country town, delightful and inexhaustibly interesting as he makes them, acquire a new and an intensely dramatic meaning when we remember what the game was (he never forgot) of which these trifles were the moving pieces. He was playing desperately for sanity, and if his trifles had failed him he was lost. He was saved, I believe, by his capacity for pleasure. ' I never,' he says, ' received a *little* pleasure from anything in my life.'

We are painfully reminded by Cowper's hobbies and employments of the devices of prisoners sentenced to confinement for life. ' The mind,' he writes, ' long wearied with the sameness of a dull dreary prospect, will gladly fix its eyes on anything that may make a little variety in its contemplations, though it were but a kitten playing with her tail.' His pets are the tame mouse of prisoners' stories, and his joinery and cage-making a homely counterpart of the hidden file and the loosened bar. They served their purpose, but a time came when they no longer occupied him, when they could not save him from the pit. ' I cannot amuse myself, as I once could, with carpenters' or with gardeners' tools, or with squirrels and guinea-pigs.' It was at this stage in his liberation that he took to writing, though even that, it seems, was accidental : it might have been fiddling. ' Perhaps had I understood music, I had never written verse, but had lived upon fiddle-strings instead.' Fortunately both for us and for him he found poetry, and especially the pains and ingenuities of it, the best remedy for his disease. An unwonted animation is observable in him, an air of confidence and purpose which surprised himself. His letters take a new tone, and when success and recognition came, and the friends who had thought him lost began to gather round him, he tasted happiness. He was like Joseph in the well, he said, and his friends were coming down into the well to see him.

It might have been hastily supposed that, living as he did, he could have little to write about. Of news, it is true, there was often little enough, but he is equally interesting when there is none. Letter-writing is a kind of game, and the best player is seldom the player with the most elaborate equipment. Cowper can make a letter out of anything. A certain privacy of station, and a spectator attitude to life, have always, in fact, been favourable to English letter-writing. Powers that might otherwise have been squandered on the public distil their essence for private ears.

Besides, things happen, even in retirement. A hare escapes. There is a fire in the village. One tries a new pill. Seeds are planted, and something amazingly comes up. Business, or what presents itself under that imposing character, finds us out. I used to wonder, says Cowper, how our antediluvian forefathers endured their seven or eight hundred years of life. ' But I think I can answer it now. I will suppose myself born a thousand years before Noah was born or thought of. I rise with the sun ; I worship ; I prepare my breakfast ; I swallow a bucket of goats' milk, and a dozen good sizeable cakes. I fasten a new string to my bow, and my youngest boy, a lad of about thirty years of age, having played with my arrows till he has stripped off all the feathers, I find myself obliged to repair them. The morning is thus spent in preparing for the chace, and it is become necessary that I should dine. I dig up my roots ; I wash them ; I boil them ; I find them not done enough ; I boil them again ; my wife is angry ; we dispute ; we settle the point ; but in the meantime the fire goes out, and must be

kindled again. All this is very amusing. I
hunt ; I bring home the prey ; with the skin
of it I mend an old coat, or I make a new one.
By this time the day is far spent ; I feel myself
fatigued, and retire to rest. Thus what with
tilling the ground and eating the fruit of it,
hunting and walking, and running, and mend-
ing old clothes, and sleeping and rising again,
I can suppose an inhabitant of the primaeval
world so much occupied, as to sigh over the
shortness of life, and to find at the end of many
centuries, that they had all slipt through his
fingers, and were passed away like a shadow.
What wonder then that I, who live in a day of
so much greater refinement, when there is so
much more to be wanted, and wished, and to
be enjoyed, should feel myself now and then
pinched in point of opportunity, and at some
loss for leisure to fill four sides of a sheet like
this ? ' See the interest on capital this letter-
writer gives ! His capital in facts might be
stowed in a sentence : ' I am busier here than
you would think.'

Sometimes he has nothing to say, and explains why, nevertheless, it entertains him to
say it. ' It is more than possible that this
may prove a blank.' But ' when I write, as

I do to you, not about business, nor on any subject that approaches to that description, I mean much less my correspondent's amusement . . . than my own. There is a pleasure annexed to the communication of one's ideas, whether by word of mouth, or by letter, which nothing earthly can supply the place of, and it is the delight we find in this mutual intercourse that not only proves us to be creatures intended for social life, but more than anything else perhaps fits us for it.' The philosophers are wrong. It is not the necessities of man that have made him gregarious, but a generous and brotherly attachment to his kind. Some characters there are, indeed, who seem to contribute nothing to society, and to have no relish for its pleasures. ' A man of this stamp passes by our window continually ; he draws patterns for the lace makers ; I never saw him conversing with a neighbour but once in my life, though I have known him by sight these twelve years ; he is of a very sturdy make, has a round belly, extremely protuberant, which he evidently considers as his best friend, because it is his only companion, and it is the labour of his life to fill it. I can easily conceive that it is merely the love of good eating

and drinking, and now and then the want of
a pair of shoes, that attaches this man so much
to the neighbourhood of his fellow mortals. . . .
He might strut about with his two thumbs
upon his hips in a wilderness ; he could hardly
be more silent than he is at Olney. . . . But
other men have something more than guts to
satisfy ; there are yearnings of the heart,
which, let philosophers say what they will, are
more importunate than all the necessities of
the body. It is not because there are no
tailors or pastry-cooks to be found upon Salis-
bury Plain that you do not choose it for your
abode, but because you are a philanthropist,—
because you are susceptible of social impressions, and have a pleasure in doing a kindness
when you can.—Witness the salmon you sent,
and the salmon you still mean to send ; to
which your mother wishes you to add a hand-
ful of prawns. . . .

'Now upon the word of a poor creature, I
have said all that I have said, without the least
intention to say one word of it when I began.
But thus it is with my thoughts :—when you
shake a crab-tree, the fruit falls.'

Like many great men Cowper liked to believe that his family came from Scotland.   Like

a very different character, the philosopher Kant, he even ventured to find his roots in the exclusive county of Fife. But I could never believe this, and there seems, in fact, to be nothing in it. There are Coopers in Fife and there are Cowpers in England, but only because there are barrels in both countries. William Cowper is an English genius, if ever there was one, and of the purest breed. Something of this was felt as soon as he found readers,—has always been felt, and is felt still. His chair is on the hearthstone of the race, and his delights are intimate and English :

Fireside enjoyments, home-bred happiness.

His fame, though it pleased him, was not without its inconveniences. People came to visit, attracted, as he says, ' by the effluvia of his genius.' Ladies sent him odes, and one of them addressed him as ' the best of men.' A Welsh attorney asked him to revise his verses. I begin to perceive, he remarks, ' that if a man will be an author, he must live neither to himself nor to his friends, so much as to others, whom he never saw nor shall see.' The most startling visit was the visit of a canvassing candidate for Parliament in the year 1784, and I quote the account of it not only because it is exhilarating in itself, but because it introduces us to the famous parlour at Olney with all the family at home. 'We were sitting yesterday after dinner,' Cowper writes to the Rev. Mr. Newton, ' the two ladies and myself, very composedly, and without the least apprehension of any such intrusion in our snug parlour, one lady knitting, the other netting, and the gentleman winding worsted, when to our unspeakable surprise a mob appeared before the window ; a smart rap was heard at the door, the boys halloo'd, and the maid announced Mr. Grenville. Puss [1] was unfortunately let out of her box, so that the candidate, with all his good friends at his heels, was refused admittance at the grand entry, and referred to the back door, as the only possible way of approach.

' Candidates are creatures not very susceptible of affronts, and would rather, I suppose, climb in at a window than be absolutely excluded. In a minute, the yard, the kitchen, and the parlour, were filled. Mr. Grenville advancing toward me shook me by the hand with a degree of cordiality that was extremely

[1] His tame hare.

seducing. As soon as he and as many more
as could find chairs were seated, he began to
open the intent of his visit. I told him I had
no vote, for which he readily gave me credit.
I assured him I had no influence, which he was
not equally inclined to believe, and the less,
no doubt, because Mr. Ashburner, the draper,
addressing himself to me at this moment, in-
formed me that I had a great deal. Supposing
that I could not be possessed of such a treasure
without knowing it, I ventured to confirm my
first assertion, by saying, that if I had any I
was utterly at a loss to imagine where it could
be, or wherein it consisted. Thus ended the
conference. Mr. Grenville squeezed me by
the hand again, kissed the ladies, and withdrew. He kissed likewise the maid in the
kitchen, and seemed upon the whole a most
loving, kissing, kind-hearted gentleman. He
is very young, genteel, and handsome. He
has a pair of very good eyes in his head, which
not being sufficient as it should seem for the
many nice and difficult purposes of a senator,
he has a third also, which he wore suspended
by a ribband from his buttonhole. The boys
halloo'd, the dogs barked, Puss scampered,
the hero, with his long train of obsequious

followers, withdrew.   We made ourselves very merry with the adventure, and in a short time settled into our former tranquillity, never probably to be thus interrupted more.'

I wished to leave you with this picture, and take my departure with the candidate.

December 8, 1926.

KINGLAKE'S EOTHEN

KINGLAKE'S *Eothen* is less read than it used to be, or than it deserves. It had a great vogue when it appeared in 1844, and its reputation is established as a Victorian classic ; but Victorian classics until lately have been cheap in the modern market. I am glad of an opportunity to recall its merits, and to recommend it to you as one of the most companionable of books. I first made its acquaintance in the excellent Oxford edition of 1906, which Mr. Hogarth edited, and it has made many journeys with me since. It is that very rare thing, a first-rate book of travel, and that still rarer thing, a book of travel that, without India paper, will go sweetly into the pocket.

' Eothen,' I should perhaps explain, is Greek, and means ' from the Dawn ' or ' from the East.' It was the title chosen by Kinglake for his narrative of a youthful journey to the Near East, from Belgrade to Constantinople, and over Syria and Palestine and part of Egypt. The time was a little less than a century ago, in the years 1834 and 1835, when the Turkish power, though badly shaken, still lay heavy and sullen on the peoples of the Balkans, before Serbia was free or Bulgaria a nation, and long, of course, before the British occupation of Egypt : though young Kinglake, with his eye for situations, foresaw even then that probability. He had been preceded, in this as in some other experiences, by an even livelier intelligence. Young Benjamin Disraeli, only three years before, had made much the same journey, and had brought back from it impressions which were to colour his whole life, and of which we feel the influence to this day. Kinglake put it all into a superb book of travel. Disraeli, after scattering it through half a dozen novels, embodied it in that bold stroke of policy which laid the foundations of British ascendancy in Egypt, and in that Act which gave final authority to the conception of an Indian Empire with the Sovereign of Great Britain at its head. So important is it that our great men should see the world, and see it young.

The ' call of the East,' as it became the fashion to describe it, was keenly felt by Kinglake's and Disraeli's generation, and by Kinglake the call of the Desert as well. It was a mixed emotion : a luxurious desire for Oriental mystery and splendour, and a more primitive, a more athletic, a more English desire for the wild life of the Desert,—to cut free for a time from respectability and top-hats, and the monotonous certainty of police protection, and take one's chance among the untamed things. Kinglake, as he glories in his freedom, spares a word of pity now and then for the poor devils at home ' presenting their compliments ' and ' requesting the honour ' and ' much regretting '—' pinioned at dinner-tables, or stuck up in ball-rooms, or cruelly planted in pews '— living, in short, ' in a state of utter respectability.' ' If a man, and an Englishman,' he says, in the chapter called ' My First Bivouac,' ' if a man, and an Englishman, be not born of his mother with a Chiffney-bit in his mouth, there comes to him a time for loathing the wearisome ways of society—a time for not liking tamed people—a time for *not* sitting in pews—a time for impugning the foregone opinions of men, and haughtily dividing truth from falsehood—a time, in short, for questioning, scoffing, and railing—for speaking lightly of the very opera, and all our most cherished institutions. It is from nineteen to two or three and twenty, perhaps, that this war of the man against men is like to be waged most sullenly. You are yet in this smiling England, but you find yourself bending your way to the dark sides of her mountains,—climbing the dizzy crags,—exulting in the fellowship of mists and clouds, and watching the storms how they gather, or proving the mettle of your mare upon the broad and dreary downs, because you feel congenially with the yet unparcelled earth. A little while you are free, and un-labelled, like the ground that you compass ; but Civilization is watching to throw her lasso ; you will be surely enclosed, and sooner or later brought down to a state of mere use-fulness—your grey hills will be curiously sliced into acres and roods and perches, and you, for all you sit so wilful in your saddle, you will be caught—you will be taken up from travel, as a colt from the grass, to be trained, and tried, and matched, and run. This in time ; but first come continental tours, and the moody longing for eastern travel : the downs and moors of England can hold you no longer ; with larger stride you burst away from these slips and patches of free land—you thread your path through the crowds of Europe, and at last, on the banks of Jordan, you joyfully

know that you are upon the very frontier of
all accustomed respectabilities.   There, on the
other side of the river (you can swim it with
one arm), there reigns the people that will
be like to put you to death, for *not* being a
vagrant, for *not* being a robber, for *not* being
armed and houseless.   There is comfort in
that—health, comfort, and strength to one
who is aching from very weariness of that
poor, dear, middle-aged, deserving, accom-
plished, pedantic, and painstaking governess,
Europe.'

You see that (whether I can read or not)
this young man can write.   You see more, that
he is not afraid to write.   It is one of the para-
doxes of Victorian publishing that his book was
refused by several publishers, and was issued
at last partly at his own expense.   In less than
eighteen months it was in its third edition,
and John Murray, we are told, spoke of the
refusal of the manuscript as the greatest lapse
of his literary judgment.

Eothen is pre-eminently a young man's book.
Kinglake was in the thirties when he wrote it,
but only twenty-five or twenty-six when he
made the journey.   There is a fine headstrong
wind of freedom blowing through it, and such

a vividness of travel that you can almost hear the crackling of the camp-fire and the jingling of the stirrup-irons. All his wits and senses are at work, for he knows that this cannot happen again ; he is youth the truant, on ticket-of-leave from civilization. The temper and character of the writer come strongly home to us on every page. ' My excuse for the book,' he says, ' is its truth. . . . My narrative is not merely righteous in matters of fact (where fact is in question), but it is true in this larger sense—it conveys, not those impressions which *ought to have been* produced upon any " well constituted mind," but those which were really and truly received at the time of his rambles, by a headstrong and not very amiable traveller, whose prejudices in favour of other people's notions were then exceedingly slight. As I have felt so have I written. . . . Now a traveller is a creature not always look- ing at sights—he remembers (how often !) the happy land of his birth—he has, too, his moments of humble enthusiasm about fire, and food—about shade and drink ; and if he gives to these feelings anything like the promin- ence which really belonged to them at the time of his travelling, he will not seem a very good teacher. . . . But it seems to me that this egotism of a traveller, however incessant, however shameless and obtrusive, must still convey some true ideas of the country through which he has passed. His very selfishness . . . compels him to observe the laws of perspective ;— he tells you of objects, not as he knows them to be, but as they seemed to him. The people, and the things that most concern him personally, however mean and insignificant, take large proportions in his picture, because they stand so near to him. He shows you his Dragoman, and the gaunt features of his Arabs—his tent—his kneeling camels—his baggage strewed upon the sand :—but the proper wonders of the land—the cities—the mighty ruins and monuments of bygone ages, he throws back faintly in the distance. It is thus that he felt, and thus he strives to repeat, the scenes of the Elder World. You may listen to him for ever without learning much in the way of Statistics ; but, perhaps, if you bear with him long enough, you may find yourself slowly and faintly impressed with the realities of Eastern Travel.'

It is a perfect description of how the book affects its readers.

Travelling in Europe, or in Europeanised countries, is a process so temporary—it occupies, we are reminded, so small a proportion of the traveller's entire time, that his mind remains unsettled so long as the wheels are going. He is conscious of being in a provisional state, and his mind is for ever recurring to the expected end of his journey. ' It will be otherwise with you,' says Kinglake (he is speaking of 1834), ' when you travel in the East. Day after day, perhaps week after week, and month after month, your foot is in the stirrup. To taste the cold breath of the earliest morn, and to lead or follow your bright cavalcade till sunset through forests or mountain passes, through valleys and desolate plains, all this becomes your MODE OF LIFE, and you ride, eat, drink, and curse the mosquitoes as systematically as your friends in England eat, drink, and sleep. If you are wise you will not look upon the long period of time thus occupied in actual movement, as the mere gulf dividing you from the end of your journey, but rather as one of those rare and plastic seasons of your life, from which, perhaps, in after times, you may love to date the moulding of your character.' The moral philosophy of travel was never better expounded.

Kinglake's companion fell ill on the road to Constantinople, and, with the Plague about, gave his party much anxiety. There he lay upon a quilt on the floor, without the humblest sort of comforts, ' and (sad to say) without the consolation of a friend, or even a comrade worth having.' Where, then, we ask, was Kinglake ? Was he not his friend, his comrade ? Listen : for this goes deep. ' I have a notion,' says our author, ' that tenderness and pity are affections occasioned in some measure by living within doors.' (You see what he is heading for ? and what a cold tap of truth he can set running ?). ' Certainly, at the time I speak of,' he goes on, ' the open-air life which I had been leading, or the wayfaring hardships of the journey, had so strangely blunted me, that I felt intolerant of illness, and looked down upon my companion, as if the poor fellow, in falling ill, had betrayed a want of spirit : I entertained, too, a most absurd idea—an idea that his illness was partly affected. You see that I have made a confession : this I hope—that I may hereafter look charitably upon the hard, savage acts of peasants, and the cruelties of a " brutal " soldiery. God knows that I strived to melt myself into common charity, and to put on a gentleness which I could not feel ; but this attempt did not cheat the keenness of the sufferer.' There must be many who in their periods of greatest fitness in the late War made Kinglake's discovery, and have wondered since at that primitive hardness. We should remember this when we read history.

Eothen, in one view of it, is a presentation of Near Eastern scenes and types, and modern authority assures us that the strange specimens of humanity which Kinglake presents are true types—true then, and true now. This young man, it appears, with all his air of irresponsibility, had an eye for essentials, for the things that do not change. A hundred years have hardly antiquated his sketches ; you need only push them a little further East. ' Reading *Eothen*,' says Mr. Hogarth, ' the modern traveller in the Near East is never moved to criticize . . . to say tolerantly, that this may, or may not, have been so two or three generations ago, but will nowhere be found now— still less that so and so could never have been. If not in Belgrade of the twentieth century, none the less in every Ottoman and Arab town, even in Constantinople and Cairo, you may yet walk (as Kinglake describes it) on soft streets of immemorial dust feeling all the oppression of that silence which " follows you still," and of a patient lack-lustre stare, still regarding you as " an unaccountable, uncomfortable work of God, that may have been sent for some good purpose—to be revealed hereafter." '

So the strangeness of the East, in spite of some recent transformations, looks on at the intrusive strangeness of the West. The Golden Horn is now bridged, and new forces rule in Turkey, but every visitor to Constantinople must feel that Kinglake has touched the heart of its melancholy and sinister magnificence. 'Nowhere else does the sea come so home to a city. . . . The stormy bride of the Doge is the bowing slave of the Sultan —she comes to his feet with the treasures of the world—she bears him from palace to palace—by some unfailing witchcraft, she entices the breezes to follow her, and fan the pale cheek of her lord—she lifts his armed navies to the very gates of his garden—she watches the walls of his Serail—she stifles the intrigues of his Ministers—she quiets the scandals of his Court—she extinguishes his rivals and hushes his naughty wives all one by one.'

This, you will agree, is no common writer, and no ordinary sight-seer. I recall, and recommend to you, among other good things in the panorama of his book, the night ride through the great Serbian forest on the way to Adrianople—the tall oaks closing round the party ' as grim as an army of giants with a thousand years' pay in arrears.' Or the narrative, in the seventeenth chapter, of his journey from Gaza to Cairo, which gives, says a modern explorer, ' a better understanding of the Desert and of Desert life than any other description half so brief.' He visited the ' Holy Cities,' and took the opportunity (which indeed was forced upon him) of distinguishing by their countries of origin the international collection of pilgrim fleas for which such places are famous. He noted, also, and doubtless exemplified, when religious feeling broke out in riot, ' that peculiar air of serenity and gratification with which an English gentleman looks on at a row.' Perhaps the finest single tale is his story of the humours of Cairo under the Plague. He, a

mad Englishman, madder than most, insisted
on going through with it, and by scorning all
risks saved his nerve, and for that reason, no
doubt, his life. He made an interesting discovery
there. Every traveller about the world, wher-
ever he may go, finds a Scot installed. Kinglake found him in Cairo : Osman Effendi, a
Scottish drummer-boy, taken prisoner in 1807
at the defeat of General Fraser near Rosetta.
Osman, in 1835, was a personage in Egypt, a
Mohammedan notable, but nothing could
burn out of him his native love of all that was
Scottish. ' In vain men called him Effendi—in
vain he swept along in eastern robes—in vain
the rival wives adorned his hareem ; the joy of
his heart still plainly lay in this, that he had
three shelves of books, and that the books were
thoroughbred Scotch—the Edinburgh this, the
Edinburgh that, and above all, I recollect he
prided himself upon the " Edinburgh Cabinet
Library ".' Poor Osman was less fortunate
than Kinglake. He died of the Plague.

I have kept the best to the end (or is it too
well known to bear keeping ?) : the great
symbolic interview, in an early chapter,
between the Eastern and the Western mind.
If *Eothen* had nothing else in it worth reading

it would survive for that conversation alone,—
between Mr. Mudcombe of the Mudcombes
of Mudcombe Park, J.P. designate for Bed-
fordshire, and the Pasha of the everlasting
Pashalik of Karagholookoldour.   It should
be read much more than once, and read aloud.

December 22, 1926.

THE HUMOUR OF CHARLES LAMB

THE first thing that occurred to me about this Talk, as it is called, was how Lamb would have hated it ! He lived for his friends, and avoided publicity. And yet,—I don't know. Has anybody worth speaking to ever read the *Essays of Elia*—or his still more wonderful private Letters—without loving Charles Lamb ? I shall consider this a talk among friends.

Lamb was not a professional author, and that is a comfort. He never in his life got up a subject in order to write about it. He wrote for fun, and you can trust every word he says. Most of his working life was spent in business. He was for thirty-three years an accounting clerk in the East India House, and retired on a pension just a century ago this year. He had found it difficult at first to settle to the desk. ' I notice, Mr. Lamb,' said one of his superiors, ' that you come very late every morning.' ' Yes,' said Lamb, stammering as was his habit, ' but see how early I go ! '

He was young then : here is a later portrait. Anyone in the habit of traversing Covent Garden, says Barry Cornwall, by merely extend-

ing his walk a few yards into Russell-street,
' might have noted a small spare man, clothed
in black, who went out every morning and
returned every afternoon, as regularly as the
hands of the clock moved towards certain
hours. You could not mistake him. He was
somewhat stiff in manner, and almost clerical
in his dress ; which indicated much wear.
He had a long, melancholy face, with keen,
penetrating eyes ; and he walked with a short,
resolute step, City-wards. He looked no one
in the face for more than a moment, yet contrived to see everything as he went on. No
one who ever studied the human features could
pass by without recollecting his countenance ;
it was full of sensibility and it came upon you
like a new thought, which you could not help
dwelling upon afterwards ; it gave rise to
meditation and did you good. This small
half-clerical man was—Charles Lamb.'

Not much sign, you would say, of Humour
here ? Where are the rosy gills, the well-fed
paunch, of the advertised Humourist ? Ah,
but there is a Humour that is shy and self-
respecting. That melancholy face—how often
it conceals a Humourist ! For Humour may
be the flower of gravity. Lord Tennyson is

not generally considered an authority on Humour, but he knew this. ' I dare not tell,' he said, ' how high I rate Humour, which is generally most fruitful in the highest and most solemn human spirits. Dante is full of it. Shakespeare, Cervantes, and almost all the greatest have been pregnant with this glorious power. You will find it even in the Gospel of Christ.' The humour of Lamb is of this kind : rooted in tenderness and suffering. There had been tragedy in his family—madness—his sister killed her mother and was shut up. Lamb undertook the care of her, and for the rest of his life (he was then twenty-one) they were never separated.

There is a principle of unity in every life, if we could find it. The principle of Lamb's, jest as he might, was self-sacrifice, and that rarest sort of self-sacrifice which refuses to be praised, or even mentioned. If you had said to Lamb, ' How I admire the way you have sacrificed your life for your sister ! ', he would have cut you dead.

The humour of a man is best seen among his friends. One of Lamb's indulgences after office-hours was to have little receptions in his rooms. ' Like other great men, I have a public day, cribbage and pipes.' It was all done on a few shillings ; but the best talk in London was to be heard there, and the best jokes. Lamb was in his glory, blurting out the finest things. The company assembled was odd and various : a ragged regiment, he calls them, though some of them are now famous enough. They were all *characters*, like their host : men, that is to say, who could be depended on to be themselves in any circumstances. When a new-comer arrived, they didn't ask, ' Has he written anything ? ' ; they were above that pedantry. They waited to see what he could do. If he could take a hand at piquet, he was welcome. If he *liked* anything, if he took snuff heartily, it was sufficient. He would understand by analogy the pungency of other things. How they punned ! Lamb has come down to us as a great punster. It was the age of puns— a form of humour now gone out. To say to an unsuspecting tradesman walking along carrying a hare : ' Excuse me, Sir, but is that your own hare or a wig ? '—this was to achieve fame. Lamb excelled at the sport ; but the humour of his writings is something very different. It is delicate and profound, the prose poetry of humour. I cannot hand

you it in spoonfuls; you must go to the
Essays and the Letters for yourselves, and
bathe in it. Read him again, at this suit-
able season, on *Roast Pig* : on *crackling* : on
Christmas. Read him anywhere : he will
never fail you.

In company, when the glass went round,
Lamb was sometimes reckless. He once pulled
Wordsworth's nose, which by its size and shape
offered excellent opportunities ; shouting at
him, 'You old Lake poet! You rascally
Poet!' What a scene! It is unaccount-
ably omitted from our Histories of Literature.
Was Wordsworth, then, offended? outraged?
Wordsworth, proudest and most dignified of
men, was nothing of the kind. All he said was,
'Charles! My *dear* Charles!'—like an in-
dulgent aunt. Wordsworth knew his man,
and thought him one of the best men, for sheer
goodness, who ever lived.

Living, as I do, in Oxford, I cannot resist
Lamb's portrait of the 'Gentle Giantess' of
this place—the widow Blackett, whom he
once saw here—'the largest female he ever
had the pleasure of beholding' :

With more than man's bulk her humours and
occupations are eminently feminine. She sighs,

—being six foot high. She languisheth,—being two feet wide. She worketh slender sprigs upon the delicate muslin,—her fingers being capable of moulding a Colossus. She sippeth her wine out of a glass daintily,—her capacity being that of a tun of Heidelberg. . . . Softest and largest of thy sex, adieu ! By what parting attribute may I salute thee, last and best of the Titanesses,—Ogress, fed with milk instead of blood ; not least, or least handsome, among Oxford's stately structures,—Oxford, which, in its deadest time of vacation, can never properly be said to be empty, having thee to fill it !

How Lamb enjoys it all, rolling in pure extravagance like a pony in a meadow ! I have always fancied that the Stout Lady in Gilbert's *Patience* owes something to our Oxford widow.

The poet Cowper, on whom also the shadow of insanity had fallen, attributed the playfulness of his letters to the need of dodging Despair. ' The effort we make to get rid of a load is usually violent in proportion to the weight of it. . . . Perhaps you remember the Undertakers' dance in the *Rehearsal*, which they perform in crape hat-bands and black cloaks, to the tune of " Hob or Nob," one of the sprightliest airs in the world. Such is my fiddling, and such is my dancing.' A vein of wildness in Lamb's humour may be put down, perhaps, to the same cause. But even in youth, when despair comes easy, and his family miseries were still fresh, his happy wisdom dispelled the darkness. He had a younger friend, much given to unreasonable melancholy, and this is how he admonishes him at twenty-three :

> My dear Robert,
>
> One passage in your letter a little displeased me. . . . You say that ' this world to you seems drained of all its sweets ! ' At first I had hoped you only meant to insinuate the high price of Sugar ; but I am afraid you meant more. O Robert, I don't know what you call sweet. Honey and the honeycomb, roses and violets are yet in the earth. The sun and moon yet reign in Heaven, and the lesser lights keep up their pretty twinklings. Meats and drinks, sweet sights and sweet smells, a country walk, spring and autumn, follies and repentance, quarrels and reconcilements, have all a sweetness by turns. Good humour and good nature, friends at home that love you, and friends abroad that miss you, you possess all these things, and more innumerable, and these are all sweet things. . . . You may extract honey from everything ; do not go agathering after gall. The Bees are wiser in their generation than the race of sonnet writers and complainers. . . . I assure you I find this world a very pretty place.

And so it is, when so sweet a temper can survive its bitterness.

Like another great humourist and great Londoner, Charles Dickens, Lamb loved children, and looked up to childhood. The best novels of Dickens and the best Essays of Lamb are founded on memories of childhood, and the world to both of them seemed too grown up. 'Why must everything smack of man and mannish?' says Lamb. 'Is childhood dead?' He had a horror of looking senior, or like anything important, and was once visibly perturbed when some school children took off their caps to him. 'They take me for a visiting governor,' he muttered, and it worried him. The *Essays of Elia*, like the novels of Dickens, have done much to improve the world for children. Children loved Lamb. There is a story of Mrs. Hazlitt's little girl stopping people in the street to tell them—'*Mr. Lamb is coming to see us!*' One exception only he made, characteristic of a bachelor : he ruled out Squalling Babies ; and on a certain occasion in company, while the air was rent with infant cries, stood up and proposed the health of the 'm-m-much ca-calumniated good King

Herod.' But the noise of children at play—
not over near—was music to him ; and he liked
to hear it when he was writing.

One of the terrors of his life was being left
alone with a sensible well-informed man who
did not know him. He was of that select
minority (the salt of the earth) who if the
sun rose in the West would observe nothing
unusual. If a subject did not interest him, he
left it alone, and in everything that related to
science was ' a whole Encyclopaedia behind
the rest of the world.' That repulsive young
gentleman, Macaulay's schoolboy, would have
thought very meanly of Lamb. His Essays
are a continual confession of his shortcomings
—in music, among the rest. ' Reader,' he
begins an Essay, ' I have no Ear ' ; and yet
he had ' weathered,' as he says, many a
' Mozartian storm.' He wrote some verses
on the subject, which provoked his sister Mary
to a reply ; and I should like to repeat them
to you. Here is Lamb :

> Some cry up Haydn, some Mozart,
> Just as the whim bites ; for my part,
> I do not care a farthing candle
> For either of them, or for Handel.—
> Cannot a man live free and easy,
> Without admiring Pergolesi ?

Or thro' the world in comfort go,
That never heard of Dr. Blow ?
So help me God, I hardly have ;
And yet I eat, and drink, and shave,
Like other people, if you watch it,
And know no more of Stave or Crotchet,
Than did the Primitive Peruvians,
Or those old ante-queer-Diluvians . . .
The devil, with his hoof so cloven,
For aught I care, may take Beethoven ;
And, if the bargain does not suit,
I 'll throw him Weber in to boot . . .
I would not go four miles to visit
Sebastian Bach (or Batch, which is it ?) ;
No more I would for Bononcini.
As for Novello, or Rossini,
I shall not say a word to grieve 'em,
Because they 're living, so I leave 'em.

Here is Mary's retort, addressed to their musician friend, Novello :

The reason why my brother 's so severe
Vincentio, is—my brother has no *ear* ;
And Caradori her mellifluous throat
Might stretch in vain to make him learn a note.
Of common tunes he knows not anything,
Nor *Rule Britannia* from *God Save the King.*
He rail at Handel ! He the gamut quiz !
I 'd lay my life he knows not what it is.
His spite at music is a pretty whim—
He loves not it because it loves not him.

What a brother and sister ! She is Bridget Elia in the Essays—he could not leave her out.

Lamb retired from business at fifty, and his retirement, as so often happens, was not altogether a success. He had long looked forward to it (' O for a few years between the grave and the desk ! '), and yet, when it came, it seemed to come too suddenly. Anyone who is thinking of giving up work should read his essay, ' The Superannuated Man,' and his letters of that time. With all the day before you, and no duties, why get up ? An insidious question. ' I walk about,' he says, ' not to and from.' He tried dropping in to his old room in the counting house ; but there was another coat on his peg—he didn't like it— things were changed. He even took to going to the British Museum : ' it is a sort of Office to me ; hours 10 to 4, the same.' Perhaps, like many others who have sighed to be liberated, he would have been happier in the old harness.

There is a sentence of Bacon's which everybody knows, in which he divides books into three classes : Books to be tasted, Books to be swallowed, and Books—a small number—to be chewed and digested. I never greatly admired this sentence. Why must our reading be expressed in terms of the gullet, and mastication, and the gastric juices ?   I have a prettier figure,—that some Books should be nodding acquaintances, that others should be visiting acquaintances, and that some few are to be loved.   The *Essays* of Bacon, for all their wisdom, are not of this third class ; the *Essays of Elia* are.

We live in hard times ; and there are men and women in my audience who are thinking, perhaps, that queer fellows who go about calling themselves Elia, and who refuse to grow up, are hardly the sort of persons to be encouraged at the present day.   Let them have no fear.   Every generation breeds its captains of industry ; but it takes centuries to make an Elia.   And moreover, I have a story for them.   Crabb Robinson, a young barrister friend of Lamb's, was once offered a case on circuit for no other reason than that the solicitor had heard he was a friend of Lamb's,—because he had read his Essays, and loved that man.   So that to be friends with Elia may actually bring trade !   It certainly brings a blessing.

December 21, 1925.